Brand Engagement

Public Relations and other techniques
to make your brand shine

Brand Engagement

Public Relations and other techniques
to make your brand shine

Wendy McWilliams

With informative chapters from respected
Australian business leaders

wmc
Public Relations

First edition published in 2013
Copyright © Wendy McWilliams 2013

Published by:
WMC Public Relations Pty Limited
PO Box 1339, Glen Waverley VIC 3150, Australia
Tel: +61 3 9803 2588 Fax: +61 3 9803 1890
Email: info@wmcpr.com.au Website: www.wmcpr.com.au

Author and book links:
www.brandengagementpr.com.au
twitter.com/wmcpr
www.facebook.com/WMC.PublicRelationsAustralia

National Library of Australia Cataloguing-in-Publication entry
Author: McWilliams, Wendy, author.
Title: Brand engagement: public relations and other techniques to make your brand shine / by Wendy McWilliams.

ISBN: 9780992300500 (paperback)

Subjects: Branding (Marketing)--Australia.
Brand name products--Australia--Marketing.
Branding consultants--Australia.
Dewey Number: 658.8270994

Printed and bound in Australia. Production: Inklink Tel: 0407 825 316
Cover design: Mik Piening, Manark   Cover image: iStockphoto.com

CONTENTS

- Gaining favourable media coverage
- Preparing media lists
- Devising news angles
- Good photography
- Exclusive or broad distribution
- Timing
- PRO TIP

- PR agencies that offer advertising
- Ad agencies that offer public relations
- Testimonials
- Credibility
- Advertorials
- Full control or partial control
- PR can be more cost effective
- PRO TIP

Introduction

The spark to write this book came after the public relations company I established in 1992, WMC Public Relations, turned 20.

It jolted me into thinking about everything that I had learnt since my first job in PR and all my past experiences that are now woven into my professional makeup.

I thought it was time to share what I know with small to medium sized enterprises so that they may be helped in establishing and growing their brand, that it engages their stakeholders and continues to shine.

To enhance my chapters that cover PR tactics, I have been very fortunate to have eight guest authors who have written a chapter on their speciality and I owe them enormous thanks. They are:

Wendy Berry	Kevin Cahalane
Stefan Kazakis	Melanie Kydd
Roger La Salle	Jim Stewart
Danielle Storey	Brenda Thomson

The City of Melbourne has generously allowed me to reproduce a significant public relations program it devised and implemented, and for which it won a 'Highly Commended' in the PRIA's Golden Target Awards.

The purpose of this book is to assist you when working *on* your business. I hope it helps your business grow and prosper and adds enjoyment to your working week.

Wendy McWilliams

Foreword

I am excited to be writing the foreword for Brand Engagement, a book that has been long overdue and is sure to be well-thumbed by anyone who wants practical advice on promoting and developing their brand.

It has been brought to us by one of Australia's true brand professionals who has impeccable credentials and runs on the board to prove it, Wendy McWilliams.

I first met Wendy while working as the Market Development Manager for Emerging Products at Hewlett-Packard (HP). Wendy had a strong understanding of HP from her days as an executive at global public relations powerhouse Hill & Knowlton and then through her own business, WMC Public Relations.

I had a portfolio of new products and brands and because they were emerging, HP was not prepared to spend big advertising dollars. However, I had a great management team that gave me, "this new guy from Apple", entrepreneurial license to be creative and do things a little differently to what HP had done in the past. Our aim was to build the awareness and brand of these new products and ideas. Public relations was a core strategy and Wendy was an integral part of the success of the HP Emerging Products team.

From here, Wendy moved with me when I took over the market development of HP's commercial PC and notebook computers, which we took to number one in market share.

In my working life, I have been fortunate to work for organisations that take their brand seriously. My first role was with accounting and advisory firm KPMG, which continues to protect its brand strongly in the area of professional services. I also worked for brand powerhouses Apple and Hewlett-Packard. Two very different brands but each has remained true to its core values.

In more recent times I had the opportunity to work alongside some amazing creative people in my role as Senior Partner in the iconic Australian agency Mojo, or Publicis Mojo as it was known globally. At Mojo I was privileged to work with brands such as Telstra, Hertz, Microsoft and Nike and be part of the core team who launched Jetstar for Qantas. This experience gave me a new perspective on what a brand is and how it is created: it lives 365 days a year in 360-degree communication channels because a brand is not static, people are constantly engaging with it.

Most recently I have been involved on a global basis with sales effectiveness organisation Miller Heiman, which also takes their brand seriously. Miller Heiman has developed significant intellectual property in the form of tools, processes and strategies to drive the top line revenue of organisations in the business to business space. One of the key strategies they introduced a few years ago was to link the organisation back to its co-founder, Bob Miller, an iconic figure in US business today. They invited Bob back to the business as an advisor to ensure that while it continued to evolve, it still remained true to the core value of the founders.

My advice is always that your brand messages must be consistent whether you are advertising, posting on a social media channels, using PR (as Wendy does so well), running an event, making a sales presentation or doing a direct/interactive campaign.

When I started my own business, I took branding as seriously as the global companies mentioned above, working hard on my personal brand. This is when I re-engaged with Wendy again on a professional basis to assist building the 'Rob Hartnett' name on the speaking circuit as a sales, marketing and leadership speaker. This resulted in me speaking to audiences from Shanghai to Seattle and appearing on radio and TV, most recently as a 'Sales Expert' on *Kochies Business Builders* on Channel 7.

I believe your personal brand is the most important thing you have. It does not matter whether you are a start up, small business owner, senior executive building a corporate career or retired executive looking to sit on some boards or become a mentor, your personal brand must be constantly evolving and growing and be protected above all else.

As I developed my own business and new brand for Selling Strategies International, I also developed an additional 'Rob Hartnett' brand tied to this company and have worked hard to ensure consistency between the two.

A key piece of wisdom I can share here is that no matter what strategy you use to build your brand you must measure its results and you must park your ego. If a strategy you have does not work and the idea your teenage daughter has does, then abandon yours and go with hers. Be sure to let her know too!

Wendy's book, Brand Engagement, is a goldmine of information for anyone responsible for managing their brand. Keep it handy for everyday reference. You don't have to read it from start to finish; pick the most relevant chapter for you today and start there. Make sure you also refer to the PRO TIPs that are included at the end of each chapter.

I wish Wendy had written this book ten years ago; it would have been invaluable to me. Fortunately it is written now, so seize the opportunity. Read it, but more importantly, take action and put these strategies and ideas to work in your business and personal lives today!

Rob Hartnett
Managing Director
Selling Strategies International   Melbourne 2013
www.sellingstrategies.com.au
www.linkedin.com/rhartnett
www.facebook.com/sellingstrategies
www.youtube.com/robhartnettlive

About the Author

Wendy McWilliams, MPRIA

Wendy McWilliams established WMC Public Relations Pty Limited in 1992 after she saw the need for a proactive, flexible and cost-effective PR company that delivered a personal level of service.

More than 20 years later, scores of businesses in Australia and overseas have benefitted from the broad range of services provided by Wendy and her team.

Many people have inspired Wendy over her career in public relations, which commenced in London. During the six years she lived in London, Wendy gained considerable experience in a number of PR and advertising agencies. Wendy also had a stint working in Toronto for a few months, but when winter approached and thoughts of being snowed in were on the radar, she hot-footed it back to London.

Upon her return to Australia, Wendy joined Eric White Associates in Melbourne; Eric White being the 'father' of public relations in Australia. EWA as it was known was later taken over by one of the world's largest PR firms, Hill & Knowlton, which was later acquired by JWT Group (J. Walter Thompson). WPP Group, the world's largest communications services group, acquired JWT in 1987 along with Hill & Knowlton.

After the experience of working in such a conglomerate, Wendy moved to Sydney with her husband Ray, and over a four-year period was an Account Executive with two different PR agencies on the North Shore. Two years were spent with Pressed Image, which specialised in the IT industry, and two years with Tymson Communications.

Wendy continued to learn a great deal during these years but it was time to return 'home' to Melbourne. Following invitations from a couple of her former Melbourne clients, Wendy decided to set up her own consultancy, and continued to deliver a comprehensive range of PR services. It wasn't long before Wendy expanded the clientele adding many household names to WMC PR's client list.

Relationships are extremely valuable to Wendy, with her first client back in 1992, still "on the books" and considered a friend as well as a client. If one thing stands out with Wendy, it is the long term relationships and business associations she is proud of. For example, one city council in Melbourne's eastern suburbs has commissioned Wendy and her team to produce its business-to-business newsletter since 1997.

Today, Wendy is a contributor and mentor to many micro business owners, helping them to work through issues and grow their business.

Outside of work, Wendy's other passions are birdwatching, squash and golf. While Wendy will probably never get to reach the magic number of seeing 700 or more species of birds in Australia, 600 or maybe even 650 is a distinct possibility. This hobby has introduced Wendy to a wonderful eclectic mix of people who are passionate about the environment and saving native habitats.

All profits donated

It is to this end that Wendy wants to make a difference. The profit from the sale of this book will be donated to help the Orange-bellied Parrot. Until further notice this will be to the Orange-bellied Parrot Recovery Fund, which is helping to stop this wonderful bird from becoming extinct. More information about this bird can be found at www.birdlife.org.au/projects/orange-bellied-parrot-recovery

Wendy thanks her husband Ray McWilliams for his contribution in helping to bring this book to fruition; to friend Roslyn McMaster for her contribution in reading it several times prior to publishing; and graphic designer Mik Piening for his stunningly attractive design of the book's cover, for his input on the chapter on implementing a new corporate identity and for being a valuable part of Wendy's and WMC PR's team for more than 15 years.

How to Use This Book

After you have read the book through once, I hope you will always have it near to hand and use it regularly as a reference tool for when you are working *on* your business.

The contents pages provide detailed information about what each chapter contains, so that if you are considering a competition or giveaway, for example, you can turn straight to that chapter and get the information you require.

And if you are struggling to get inspiration for your next press release, check out the chapters on Publicity and Promotion and What is News?

The chapters by the guest authors contain a host of valuable gems that cover a wide range of essential business processes, so these too can be used for your ongoing reference as needed.

I would encourage you to visit the websites of each guest author's business, bookmark them and sign up for blogs and e-newsletters that they may issue. Most have social media links, so why not connect with them to ensure you don't miss out on the wisdom they are prepared to share with you?

Also, please go to www.wmcpr.com.au and register to be advised when a new blog has been published on the WMC Public Relations website, which is approximately every month.

I hope this book helps your brand shine and I welcome any comments you may have. Please post these at www.facebook.com/WMC.PublicRelationsAustralia

Chapter 1

Publicity and Promotion

Publicity and promotion is the most widely implemented PR tactic: gaining favourable coverage in the wide variety of online and offline media including radio and television.

Before setting out to plan a media relations campaign, it's important to know what media or blogs your target audiences are interested in and reading. Create a list of the ones you want to focus on and target.

If you don't know, do some research to find out. For example, if you are a boutique winemaker wanting to launch your latest vintage release, your customers and potential customers would probably read the weekly food and drink lift-outs and columns in the metro dailies and weekend papers/magazines along with web sites. Then there are numerous glossy magazines and influential freelance writers and bloggers, such as The Wine Punter, who specialise in the wine industry.

The editors, journalists and self publishers who write news stories and feature articles on any particular subject are constantly looking for fresh material to write about. They can't possibly source every story line themselves and they invariably welcome contributions and submissions from people who know what they are talking about as long as the information relates to their audience.

In attempting to gain publicity for your brand you need to find an angle to your news that will resonate with the journalist you are trying to sell (pitch) the story to. Most editors, journalists and reporters will receive hundreds of pitches every week, so you have to cut through the clutter and make your subject line, heading and opening paragraph stand out. For starters, make sure you personalise the email.

Just sending a press release announcing the release of a new vintage won't generate much attention unless it's Penfolds Grange or similar.

You need to find a unique aspect to the story: perhaps the wine comes from vineyards that have an unusual history; perhaps the winemaker is the youngest/oldest in the country; or perhaps it has won a prestigious award. Look hard and try and find a story around the 'news', ideally one with a human interest angle.

Having good photographs are essential. While straight product shots of the bottles of wine are necessary, think about tying the photo to the person or story that supports the 'news' item.

With a new product such as wine, taste is obviously an important criterion. Therefore, samples and tasting notes should be provided to the editor, journalist or blogger. Perhaps you could arrange for them to taste the wine at a well known restaurant with matching food?

Distribution – extensive or exclusive

If the news story is a strong one, I would definitely distribute the media release to all the media who you would expect to be interested in it. If it isn't then consider giving it to one or two media on an exclusive or semi-exclusive basis. This way you are guaranteed coverage and you may even end up the lead/front page story.

Timing is another important factor to be considered because some media won't want to be seen as being late with the news. For example, if one publication runs the story and a competing magazine receives the information past its deadline, they are unlikely to run it unless they can get a different angle. So make sure you distribute the information fairly. Note that the monthly 'glossies' work three months ahead, whereas weekly lift-outs or columns in the metro dailies usually work two to three weeks ahead.

Being even-handed in distribution is less of an issue now as nearly all print publications have websites and most have e-newsletters, as everyone is hungry for news on a day-to-day basis.

Before you send information to the journalist or editor, read and be familiar with the publication, column or website of the media you are targeting. Know what their interests are, any topical issues they are following and their style so that your covering letter (email) can be tailored to them and their audiences.

PRO TIP: The majority of media prefer to receive 'the pitch' via email. If you are offering it exclusively to them, do follow up in a day or two. If it was a widely distributed media release, don't phone them asking if they plan to run a story, it's wasting your time and theirs.

Chapter 2

PR versus Advertising

The public relations versus advertising debate is a perennial one, compounded by the rise of social media and other techniques that are employed by both professions.

This is a complex subject so this chapter will just cover what I believe are a few salient points to remember when considering PR and/or advertising in the marketing campaign for your brand.

Today, most advertising agencies have their own PR team or sister PR agency because they see the benefits of offering both services to their clients. Likewise, most PR agencies provide advertising services, particularly if the client has a limited advertising budget.

PR provides a platform to build brand credibility whereas advertising can build brand awareness.

Third party endorsements are one of the favoured ways to create credibility and are used extensively by PR departments. It is now an often-used strategy by advertising agencies.

Today, it is quite common to see testimonial advertisements. However, you can't get away from the fact that the company paid for the ad to be there. With PR, the endorsement is run by the media source who has checked (we hope!) the statements and publishes at their expense because they think it is a good story. So on the credibility stakes, PR wins hands down.

4

PR is also ahead when it comes to editorials, which by their very name mean they are published at no charge. Of course, the story has to be newsworthy or have other merits for it to be published, but when the cost of a full page advertisement for the same space is considered, the benefits are obvious.

Quite a number of industry publications offer advertisers free editorial in return for running an advertisement and don't require the word 'advertorial' on top of their editorial. Make sure you ask if this is available and if it can be product or company focused. If not, they may accept an educational, opinion or thought leadership piece instead.

Advertising does provide control because you get what you want and what you've paid for. This is crucial if you have an event and want to promote it ahead of time. Advertising is guaranteed and if done effectively will generate leads, members, visitors or whatever else you want to attract.

PR can provide some degree of control: for example, if a magazine or newspaper sponsors an award or event, they usually guarantee to give it coverage before, during and after. This means that if you enter an award and do well, or attend an event, you know that your company will be promoted.

Advertising can be expensive whereas a PR program is usually much less. The main reason for this is the space costs or airtime involved with each advertisement.

PR primarily relies on editorial, which can be continually repurposed, enhanced and added to in order for new content to be created.

Advertising allows a company to get really creative in its approach, whereas PR relies to an extent on the medium it is using to communicate its messages. However, PR campaigns are now utilising social media to add many creative elements that were previously not as accessible.

And of course advertising can continually promote a brand's image, whereas this is much harder with PR. The sports industry has got this down pat with sponsors logos now appearing on collars and helmets – as close to the person's face as possible – so that when players, coaches or racing car drivers are interviewed on television, the sponsor's logo is shown to the hundreds of thousands of people watching.

Learning from this, be creative in your PR photography and ensure the company logo is visible, even if blurred, in the executive, company or product photo.

PRO TIP: I can't say it any better than Sir Richard Branson, who spoke at an Adelaide Business Chicks breakfast in May 2013. "The head of PR is perhaps one of the most important people in a company ... They are critical for managing the brand and save millions in advertising; people talking about your company is much more important than anything."

Chapter 3

Unleash the Power of Your Customers
by Stefan Kazakis

One of the greatest challenges we face today is the speed that things get done and the lack of time to genuinely care or even do them right.

Relationships are made at transactional speed, often leading to win/lose results. In the world of business, customers are getting angry and complaining; service providers are getting frustrated to the point that they are resenting and walking away from their businesses.

Countless small businesses promise something to their customers and then fail to deliver. The cause: a less than aligned team culture and inferior training that compromises their employees' good intentions.

Too many business owners and teams are drawn to the quick fix and the cheaper option. Lack of long term strategy is creating long term growth issues. Everyone is in a hurry for success and fame. The problem is that we are not committing the time and profits (if we have them) to the fundamentals that ensure we are unleashing the power of our 'A' grade customers.

The result is that over 90 per cent of small businesses are facing a customer loyalty crisis.

How do we unleash the power of our customers?

To start with, we have to embrace ownership of the challenge and not take the position of denial that they are all 'idiots'. To unlock the vault to long term profits you need to view customers as being your principle partners in success.

Stop asking Why (aren't they doing what we want) and start asking How (can we provide what they need)?

There are four customers in every business and you need to care about all of them.

The owner is the primary customer. Second are the employees. Third are suppliers. And finally, the most important customer is the customer themselves. Most valuable are those who buy from you repeatedly and bring many more friends to you as long as you keep on delivering just a little more than you promised every time. The key to 'under promise and over deliver' is consistency. This is the foundation of your business growth.

© Stefan Kazakis

Building a reputation on service is crucial to your long term profitability. It's a critical differentiation. You must ensure that there is an ongoing investment in training and education around your value proposition for you and your team.

Then you need an understanding of the key metrics to building a raving fan base. It starts with the mantra of being aligned and non negotiable for unleashing the power of your customer 'tribe'.

It is vital to build a small business that learns to say no to its non-desired target market. You must be valued by and attractive to the target market you serve.

Get out of the way of your business

You can only truly unleash the power of your customers once you get out of the way of your business. This means playing the game in abundance not scarcity. Your aim should be to build a business where 80 per cent of your customers are ideal and contribute directly to your profits. You want to be there for them today, next year and in 10 years time.

In my experience over the past 20 plus years in building small businesses for myself and as a globally acclaimed business coach, I have come to understand the power of investing in the ideal customers — the ones your business deserves. Embrace the culture of doing whatever it takes to keep them for life.

This is the real ethos of customer service, taking action to create value for someone else with a big smile. This leads to loyal repeat business.

Even more valuable than that is referral business, which is at the heart of the most profitable businesses in the world today.

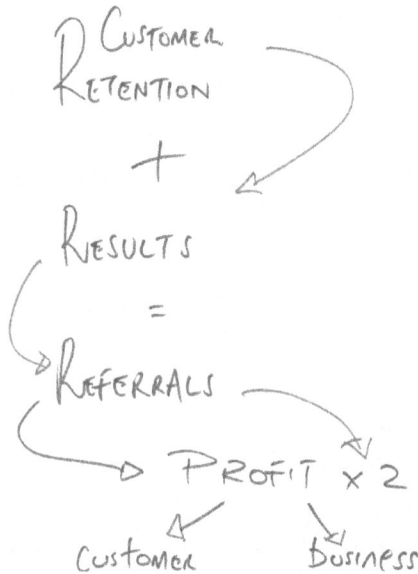

Customer Retention + Results = Referrals → Profit × 2 (Customer, Business)

© Stefan Kazakis

In saying this, there is a distinct difference between loyalty and repeat business. Loyalty is much more valuable. Loyalty is when your customers are not swayed by cheaper, better products. They continue doing business with you as they trust that your innovation will continuously be improved.

Loyal customers don't bother researching the competition or entertaining other options. Loyalty is not easily won hence it takes a very committed business to build a 'customer tribe' that is genuinely for life.

Chapter 3

Ask your customers for the brutal truth

As an exercise, I strongly suggest you pick up the phone and contact ten of your best and ten of your perceived challenging customers and ask them to give you some brutal truth about your business and how you treat them. Don't be scared, it may not be that bad! It may be not that good either. What's critical is how you respond.

Address the concerns of your most valued customers. Then do an exercise in 'tribe' identification. Determine which customers you are currently serving you wish to de-select and say to them: 'thanks but no thanks'.

Don't act on emotion. Be brave and confirm with clarity and logic which customers you will be pruning from your customer base. Make this decision based on who you want as part of your future global business. Remember to include all four relevant customers in your research.

The reality is that four out five small businesses don't make it over five years. Globally, less than seven per cent reach over $2 million in turnover in one year.

The critical skills and tools that are required to create an idea are very different to the critical skills and tools to grow the business. The miracle is in growing the business. It is imperative that you are following *Your Profit Blueprint*.

Business requires a 'scoreboard' that is brutally honest and a culture that has a bias to personal best and excellence. Both of these are moving targets. Once executed with consistency there is always a new level to strive for. If you want to be in the top 10 per cent in your industry — not the 90 per cent that are falling behind — discover and unleash the power of your 'A' grade customers.

About the author

My name is Stefan Kazakis and business is an intellectual sport. Stefan Kazakis has made a significant contribution to the growth of Melbourne business, both locally and globally, as a business owner and strategic development mentor to many small business owners. In 2011, Stefan established Board of Directors 12, a program developed for small business owners to be in an environment of progressive and strategic thinking for long term growth of their business.

W: www.boardofdirectors12.com
E: info@boardofdirectors12.com
P: +61 3 9001 0878
T: @stefankazakis
F: www.facebook.com/BoardofDirectors12
L: www.linkedin.com/in/stefankazakis
Y: www.youtube.com/user/KazakisStefan

Chapter 4

How the Correct Sales Training can Change Lives
by Wendy Berry

Do you have a great product but the thought of selling it just sends shivers up your spine?

Are you able to get in front of potential buyers but just can't seem to get them over the line?

Do you have sales people who just can't seem to perform and others who always do?

It's common amongst people and sales people to either have a fear of getting out there or if they do, their skills let them down and hence they end up on a spiral downhill. They just don't know what they don't know and frustration abides.

Great sales people have common characteristics that set them apart. They have learnt by the 'school of hard knocks' or from others who are successful.

The first thing that is evident with achievers is their charisma. People like and trust them. They have an ability to build rapport and trust. They understand they need to sell to people the way they like to buy.

This may seem obvious. Why then, doesn't everyone possess this charm if it works so well? It's learning the skills of rapport and understanding behavioural styles.

You don't need a psychometric test to determine your own style and obviously can't conduct a test on your potential customers.

It's a very simple observation of behavioural characteristics and indicators that will lead to your assessment of how people like to be dealt with.

Are they fast or slow paced? Task or relationship orientated? If they are fast paced and task focused they are called "Directors" with all the associated characteristics, job role, appearance and type of conversation.

If fast paced and relationship focused they are called "Socialisers".

Slow paced and relationship focused people are "Relators" and slow paced and task focused people are called "Thinkers".

They all like to be dealt with differently and a top sales professional will modify their own behaviour to suit.

High achievers focus on the customer at a deeper level using well thought out questions, rather than focusing on the price or the product. It's not what the product is that is important so much as what it can do to help each person's individual needs and outcomes.

It's important to ask permission to ask questions so your prospect doesn't feel interrogated and is ready to answer. Then the questions asked by a sales person to determine a potential customer's needs and to make them realise the consequences in their life/business if they don't buy, are paramount.

Some examples of questions are:
- "What do you have or use at the moment?"
- "What works well?"
- "What could be changed or improved?"
- "What else have you looked at?"
- "What was your experience?"

Once you have understood what their needs are, the questions that follow make all the difference. Some of these are:
- "What is your greatest concern with your current situation/or with buying this widget?"
- "How do you mean?"
- "Can you give me an example?"
- "Why do you think this is happening/may happen?"

A successful sales professional knows how to present solutions so that the customer can 'hear' what they are saying. Words we use influence how a customer responds. It's what we say and how we say it. We cannot, not influence.

Next we need to recognise buying signals so we know when to close the sale (confirm the outcome of our discussion), as well as how to close the sale. Also of use are trial closes so we know we are on track. These ask for an opinion rather than a decision.

What about those dreaded responses when we do ask for the order such as, "I'll think about it". Top sales people not only get fewer objections because they understand the customer, they also know how to smoke out the real objection so they can handle it professionally.

Other skills such as the ability to set and achieve goals, manage your time effectively, deal with difficult customers, negotiate, make appointments and asking for referrals and prospects are vital skills.

Making a sale is simple, but not easy. It's best to learn how.

Correct training of sales people makes the difference between them having data that they may never understand or use, and motivation and an ownership of skills and strategies that can change their lives.

About the author

Wendy Berry runs Excelerated Sales Training. Wendy's wealth of experience at all levels of business, sales and sales training and her powerful presenting skills, ensure memorable training sessions that instil lasting behavioural changes. Wendy produces impressive results by developing and enhancing skills and motivation, with an inevitable improvement to the bottom-line and undeniable success and personal growth.

W: www.wendyberry.com.au
E: wendy@exceleratedsalestraining.com.au
P: 0408 410 403
T: @TheWendyWeapon
F: www.facebook.com/wendy.berry1
L: www.linkedin.com/in/thewendyweapon

Chapter 5

Competitions and Giveaways

If you have a new product or one that has recently been enhanced or upgraded, it's worthwhile considering a giveaway as part of the media relations program and product launch.

Even service-based businesses can add competitions and giveaways to their marketing mix. For example, a company offering house cleaning services could provide a giveaway of one or more full house spring cleans. Another example could be training organisation that gives away a valuable educational program or course. Or a landscaper can give away a front garden makeover.

It's a simple equation of developing a product that you are prepared to give away and finding a relevant outlet interested in promoting it.

Most newspapers, magazines and online publications regularly run competitions and giveaways. The reach of these media will expose your brand to possibly tens of thousands of potential customers. Also, think of an organisation that has the same customers as you and perhaps they could promote your giveaway. For example, the landscaper could work with a garden centre which promotes the makeover extensively through their newsletters, website and in-store with banners and a display.

Think about holiday periods and special 'days' such as Christmas, Father's Day, Mother's Day, Easter and the beginning of the seasons, and if your product would tie in with these special times.

If liaising with a publication, contact the person who organises the giveaways, usually the marketing coordinator, and obtain the guidelines in advance of discussing your proposal. They may have some ideas or an upcoming feature where your giveaway would suit.

The guidelines will tell you what the prize level is, which is usually set at a certain level. If this is $1000, you can provide five product giveaways valued at $199 each, or if your product package is a more expensive product, one or two could be given away.

Check to see if you need to obtain a permit to run a lottery (that's what a giveaway promotion is called) as each state has different rules. Usually the publication will organise this if one is required. This government website provides links to each state's body that runs the permit system: australia.gov.au/topics/culture-history-and-sport/recreational-activities/gambling-and-lotteries

Having a good quality photograph to accompany your giveaway is important and can help sell it. If you don't want to pay for professional photography, make sure the person taking the photo knows what they are doing, especially in terms of lighting, and you end up with an attractive, high resolution photo.

You can enhance low value products

If your product is a low value item, such as a shelf-stable food item, then consider adding other relevant and more expensive products to increase the unit price.

For example, to create a hamper where low-value shortbread is to be the hero, pair with complementary items such as two expensive bone china mugs and packs of tea and coffee. This makes the hamper an attractive, higher value package. These additional items can be purchased or you may be able to have them donated or supplied at a discounted price. Be aware, however, that you want your product to have 'naming rights' so don't give away branding opportunities too lightly.

A hamper company can assemble the hamper adding colourful finishing touches before photos can be taken for promotional purposes.

When you have your product giveaway finalised, contact the competition organiser again and discuss your offer. Send through the smart photo and a short description with catchy heading and purpose for the giveaway.

As mentioned earlier, try and link your product giveaway with a topical or seasonal event for added impact. For example, good timing for the cleaning company offering a spring clean would be the beginning of September. Be aware that giveaway opportunities can be booked up months in advance, so don't leave it too late to start your planning.

Be selective in targeting the media that relate to the product being promoted and your target market. For example, the shortbread hamper giveaway could be run in food and drink sections and a spring clean could be run in newspapers and house and home media.

Some metro daily newspapers are moving to an integrated online and hard copy offer that involves advertising and editorial, which is a totally different offer. You don't have to do this. Look carefully for other straight giveaway opportunities; they are out there and most would welcome what you have to offer.

Finally, make sure you have the product or package ready to be sent before you contact the media to arrange the giveaway. If they have had a cancellation, they may slot it into their schedule within two or three weeks. Some publications prefer to have the prizes in their office before they run the promotion, others are happy for the prizes to be sent to the winners after they have been drawn.

PRO TIP: Decide in advance how much product you are prepared to give away and how much you want to spend on the total project.

Chapter 6

What is News?

When conducting a publicity and promotion campaign, you will be dealing with media who are only looking for one thing: a good story that will resonate with their audience and make them look like they are on top of the latest news and trends.

Traditional and non-traditional media want to retain their audience's attention and attract new viewers, readers and listeners.

With staff reductions in nearly every media outlet, they couldn't possibly fill their newspaper, magazine, radio or TV show, e-zine or blog without outside help, either from in-house or external PR departments.

The media want news and human interest stories; and if the story has both of these ingredients, it's even better!

PR people are trained to be alert to and dig for news and can even create news (for example, conduct research and report on the findings: refer to Chapter 9).

So what can be considered news that you can use in your business to inform the media? Here is a list to get you started...

- Milestones: first, 21st, 25th or 50th anniversary, 500th customer, 1000th or 1 millionth widget made, 20th franchise sold, reaching a $1M, $10M or $100M turnover, etc.

- Moved to new premises or opened branch offices.

- Introduced energy efficiency and sustainability measures that resulted in significant cuts to usage, gained a 6 Star Green Star rating, etc.

- Won an award or was a runner-up, finalist or nominee.

- New appointments for senior personnel such as a Chairman, CEO, Director or a national role.

- Enhancements to company infrastructure, changes to a business model, the introduction of new technology, etc.

- Commenced exporting products or established new export markets, reached an exporting milestone, etc.

- Launching new products or services, enhancements to existing products or line extensions such as a new variety or flavour.

- Publishing white papers, technical how-to sheets, etc.

- Introducing a new advertising campaign. Unless it has general interest newsworthiness, this would mainly be of interest to the advertising and marketing media.

- Developing and announcing market analysis that may be controversial or alternative to general consensus.

- Holding an event, particularly at which high profile people will be in attendance.

- Obtaining special industry certifications that are nationally or internationally recognised.

- Case studies where one of your customers has achieved significant results.

- Promotion of sponsorships, whether of the arts, sport or the community, usually provide good opportunities for publicity. In being associated with the charity or not-for-profit organisation being sponsored, ensure it is ethical and manage it so you don't end up with egg on your face. Two examples of sponsorship show how careful you must be:

  - Red Bull sponsored Austrian daredevil Felix Baumgartner, who made a record-breaking leap from the edge of space, freefalling 39 kilometres back to Earth. While it appeared risky to anyone who wasn't involved in this attempt, the reason it gained so much publicity was because it had such a high level of risk.

  - Celebrities who endorse brands such as Tiger Woods, Lance Armstrong and Oscar Pistorius have all had their sponsorships withdrawn because of their unacceptable actions.

- Finally, but by no means least, offering a substantial, unique or alternative giveaway or running an unusual competition.

A good example of this is Tourism Australia, which in 2009 ran a competition to find a 'caretaker' of Hamilton Island on the Great Barrier Reef. This really captured the world's attention with extensive media coverage at all stages of the competition including at launch, during the application process, creating a shortlist, and finally announcing the winner.

Briton Ben Southall beat over 34,000 applicants from over 200 countries to win the dream job, which required him 'to explore the islands of the Great Barrier Reef, swim, snorkel, make friends with the locals and generally enjoy the tropical Queensland climate and lifestyle'. No wonder they had so many applications!

In 2013, Tourism Australia revived this campaign and offered six dream roles for 'best job in the world competition' offering jobs such as a park ranger, outback adventurer, wildlife caretaker and 'chief funster'. This second campaign didn't attract anywhere near the same level of traditional media coverage as the first one, but it has created a buzz on the Internet, which has seen the campaign go viral and generate its own publicity.

This certainly isn't a complete list of newsworthy opportunities but it should help you start thinking about ways to promote your brand and what news can be exploited in the media.

PRO TIP: Make sure you include all news items on your website.

Chapter 7

Embedding the Innovation Culture
By Roger La Salle

Innovate or perish – the message is clear!

Innovation is the essential turbulence that drives business growth and development. The alternative is stagnation that will ultimately lead to business failure.

Recent statistics reveal that without innovation the life expectancy of a business in these fast moving times is less than ten years.

It's clear that businesses need to move with the times or risk being overtaken by competitors with new business models, new products and new services. This can even happen in businesses with high barriers to entry.

For example, 20 years ago who would have thought that Boeing would now be number two behind Airbus Industries in commercial jet aircraft, or that Apple would be seriously challenged by the likes of Samsung with their nifty tablet devices sold at half the price of the Apple equivalent?

Fast food outlets, petrol stations and convenience stores are another classic example of competition resulting in market saturation so that in many cases poorly located stores, previously profitable, are now extinct.

The question to be explored is just how to keep your business moving to be always ahead of the competition.

Embed the culture

The answer lies in the pursuit of both innovation and opportunity capture, and working to embed these into your business as a part of the culture, not just at senior management level but at all levels throughout your business.

The aim must be to embrace and embed the innovation teachings into the business so that there is ongoing benefit. Otherwise, why bother at all?

However, there is little point in just reading an interesting article, running some in-house training or inspirational 'talking head' innovation session with an expert in any field if these are just 'one shot wonders'.

Can my business do this?

In general, unless there is some particular disharmony within an organisation, most people wish to make a contribution and wish to be seen as a useful and valuable part of the team. This mindset needs to be harnessed for the good of the organisation.

To achieve this it is first necessary to train people in innovation and opportunity capture methods and then once people are equipped with tools, the next step is to form 'Innovation Circles'.

These circles should be cross functional teams that need only comprise four or five people that meet periodically, perhaps over lunchtime once every two or three weeks, where the lunch is provided courtesy of the business.

At these sessions the teams, with the guidance of a team leader, should use the innovation tools provided to explore innovations and opportunities for the business.

Experience in establishing these teams has found people are eager to become involved and to make a contribution that will be acknowledged and perhaps rewarded.

After several months of innovating in team meetings there should be a presentation by each team to senior management of the progress of their work. Perhaps annually there should be a competition for the best innovations with rewards provided to the winning teams.

Rewards need to be little more than recognition and perhaps a night out to dinner for the winning team and their partners, sponsored by the company.

What is the message?

Without innovation to drive change, most businesses will ultimately find themselves under threat, whether from competitors with better products, or those with better service approaches or new and better ways of doing business.

1.   The message must come from the top.
     - Without top down commitment, nothing will happen. Why should an employee 'go the extra mile' if the boss is not really interested?

2.   Senior management must be 'on board', interested and committed, and moreover know and understand the processes.
     - How can lower level people be engaged in the journey if senior management has no real understanding of what they are doing?

3.   Staff at many levels need to be trained in some simple thinking techniques that encompass:
     - Innovation.
     - Opportunity capture.
     - Simple and fast 'Pass – Failure' evaluation.

4.   Innovation Circles (teams) need to be formed from cross functional groups.
     - The time commitment of these people is minimal, the outputs quite remarkable.

5.   Rewards, mainly recognition, and perhaps a weekend away with partners need to be given to successful Innovation Circles.
     - Judged perhaps by half yearly or annual competitions.
     - Organisations must capture, listen to, and act upon, the ideas emanating from their staff and clients during everyday operations.

Finally

Before any attempt is made to commence the journey to inculcate an innovation/opportunity culture, there are first four essential questions that need to be addressed:
- What are you trying to achieve?
- Where are you now?
- How will you measure progress?
- What outcome defines success?

Each of these questions should be answered in a single sentence statement!

About the author

Roger La Salle, is the creator of the "Matrix Thinking"™ technique and is widely sought after as an international speaker on innovation, opportunity and business development. He is the author of four books and has been responsible for a number of successful technology start-ups. In 2005 he was appointed to the Chair of Innovation at The Queens University in Belfast. Matrix Thinking is now used in more than 26 countries and licensed to Deloitte, one of the world's largest consulting firms.

W: www.matrixthinking.com
E: rlasalle@matrixthinking.com
P: 0418 370 828
T: @RogerLaSalle
F: www.facebook.com/Roger.La.Salle.Innovation.Trainer
L: www.linkedin.com/pub/roger-la-salle/14/576/289

Chapter 8

Member Relationship Management
By Kevin Cahalane

Member Relationship Management (MRM) is a total member satisfaction solution that provides methods and systems:

- It enables you to identify, capture data, service, educate, inform and retain members utilising quality people (your team), technology (MRM also referred to as CRM) and an excellent, planned communication strategy.

- It enables you to create a unified view of each member, as an individual in their market segment and personal demographic, across the entire organisation.

- It enables you to target your marketing campaigns and your promotions more productively and cost efficiently.

- It enables you, the organisation, to maximise revenue while delivering consistent member satisfaction.

- It provides you with vital reports and analysis about your members and their activities, purchases, expectations and whatever else you require.

- It allows an organisation to enhance the experience of each member (whether it be networking, social status, education, training, support – the list is huge) as they will remain 'members for life' and become an advocate organisation.

There are three main areas where Member Relationship Management is vital:

Member recruitment

Member Relationship Management (MRM) assists you at every major level of the membership process, including acquisition of members. A quality MRM system will assist you in capturing prospective member data and building a membership sales funnel.

* Acquire prospects. Everyone has to gain prospects — lots of prospects. If your membership base is falling by 5-10 per cent a year, your prospect base should be growing by 20 per cent … minimum.

* Communicate with prospects and turn them into members. This is where the member sales funnel is so important — every good MRM system has a prospecting component.

Member retention and loyalty

MRM is crucial to member retention and engagement in seven key areas:

1. New member induction, mentoring and guidance for the first 12 months of their membership. Never assume new members will 'just fit in'. Doing so is a recipe for disaster.

2. Member complaints management systems. If you can monitor issues, you can control those issues. This is particularly relevant for larger organisations.

3. Total member service excellence across the board, where the entire team services their members. Also, an organisation can personalise its member service. For example, recognition of a volunteer member or a 10-year member, or thanking someone who refers a new member.

4. Communication (and member feedback) via email, direct mail, webinars, forums, social media, publications, 'members only' website navigation. Communication should be planned, regular and relevant.

5. Events/functions/CPD (Continuing Professional Development) and any activities that encourage member attendance and participation. A good MRM system will tell you each member's frequency of attendance, most recent activities and a financial analysis of their spending.

6. Surveys and post survey action plans. This creates future benchmarking.

7. How you market and promote your organisation to your members. This is often overlooked as an MRM tool if you get the first six points above right. However, it is vital to market and promote your organisation (particularly at renewals time) to your members.

Increase your member revenue

Not every not-for-profit organisation gains additional revenue from members. But for those who do, your primary goal here is three-fold:
1. Increase and manage your member base;
2. Increase their contact with your organisation; and
3. Increase their spend with each interaction. An MRM system will enable you to grow your revenue exponentially.

MRM helps you to build revenue if you run your contact management system efficiently and professionally.

In summary, the keys to Member Relationship Management are people, strategy and technology. Used individually, you will make some gains. Combine the three and your membership (and member revenue) will grow substantially.

About the author

Kevin Cahalane is Principal and founder of Membership Growth. Over the past 15 years, Kevin has worked with some of Australia's top associations, organisations, sporting clubs and other not-for-profit organisations. His varied roles include membership sales, service and marketing training, keynote speaking in Australia and overseas; membership development strategy; planning and execution.

W: www.membershipgrowth.com.au
E: kevin@membershipgrowth.com.au
P: +61 3 5976 8966
L: au.linkedin.com/pub/kevin-cahalane/2/150/696

Chapter 9

Surveys and Research

Surveys and other formal research can be instrumental in many types of public relations campaigns.

Both quantitative and qualitative information can help businesses plan future marketing strategies. Even the humble suggestion box is a great way to get feedback.

Whether you want information from existing customers, potential customers, employees, suppliers, shareholders, community groups or other stakeholders, surveys are an excellent tool to gauge statistics, ideas and opinions.

The information gained can be used to help your own organisation plan future growth strategies, increase loyalty among customers and employees, facilitate innovation and influence critical business decisions.

This chapter also looks at how surveys can be used to create media announcements to help promote your business.

Most business owners don't know the answers to the following questions. If you are one of these people, perhaps it is time to start finding out the answers.

Q: Do your customers know all the different facets of your business?

You may be surprised to know that some customers know you for one thing only and have no idea of the other products and services you offer.

Q: Are your customers satisfied with the products and services you deliver?

If customers are not returning, perhaps there is a specific reason that you may be able to address easily and quickly to win back the customer.

Q: How well is your brand known and respected in the marketplace?

If 100 people were given the names of five similar products including your own, where would your brand be ranked?

Q: What do your employees like and don't like about working for your company?

Unless you know, you can't do anything about it. Being an employer of choice means you attract good staff and having good staff gives you a competitive advantage.

Q: What do you know about your customers or potential customers?

If you are a service and support organisation, wouldn't it be beneficial to know the average age of equipment in use in the industry?

Q: What ideas do your employees and business partners have that can be used to create innovation in your business?

Unless you ask, you may never know. (If you haven't read Chapter 7 yet about *Embedding the Innovation Culture*, make sure you do.)

Other standard surveys include exit or post conference surveys, course/seminar evaluation surveys and 'made up' surveys.

Made up surveys

What is 'made up' I hear you ask? The results of these surveys appear regularly in the daily press and online media. It's where a company has commissioned a survey on a subject that is relevant to their business but appears purely aimed at generating publicity. The subject is usually topical or controversial so as to capture the attention of the metro daily news desk.

Once the results are in, the findings can be published and promoted through a well orchestrated PR campaign. Here are a few actual examples of these self-initiated surveys.

Example 1:

A recruitment firm conducts research (through a reputable organisation) to ascertain the percentage of employees who are happy in their job. The figure could possibly be quite low, which would have implications for the broader business community to lift their game and provide a better workplace and more suitable job position. It could even be linked to increased depression in the community if an independent authority provided added analysis. Result: ABC Recruitment gains considerable coverage, linked to a survey that it created to achieve this desired objective.

Example 2:

Global technology company, IBM, conducts a study internationally, including around 2,000 Australians, on customer loyalty. It finds that over 60 per cent of Australian consumers identify themselves as 'apathetic' in their choice of a primary retailer and that they are hungry for multi-channel innovation. The study reveals consumers are turning to mobile and social platforms, highlighting need for retailers to blend bricks and mortar with online in order to thrive.

Considerable media attention was given to the results of the study, which included quotes from an IBM executive. The media release also included quotes from the Australian National Retailers Association, which added valuable independent analysis of the study.

Example 3:

A shampoo brand commissions a survey of 1000 Australians that finds gentlemen no longer prefer blondes. Now that is a revelation that is sure to gain column inches! It also found 60 per cent of women are attracted to men with brown hair and reported that hair was a key element in sex appeal. With statistics like this and a photo of a blonde buxom woman, this brand was confident of success.

PRO TIP 1: Results of surveys are in the media every day. Brainstorm among your team to see what topic is relevant to your brand that could be of interest to the media.

PRO TIP 2: Create an infographic that summarises the results of the survey.

Chapter 10

Interviewing for Good Copy

Writing an engaging article that is going to be read from the beginning to the end is an art that can be learned. You just need to follow some basic steps.

Whether you like to read newspapers, magazines or blogs (to name a few), you would know that some articles are more engaging than others. We are all short of time so we want to be sure that the time we do spend reading stories in the media must provide value to our working or personal life.

If you want to submit material to the media, it is important to craft your words well so that readers actually want to read to the end. Be aware that readers firstly are the editors, reporters, journalists or bloggers. You need to impress these people before you can reach their subscribers and readers.

So what makes good copy? In a nutshell, it's important to have a news angle and a human interest aspect to the story. And if it is controversial as well, that's even better. Pick up any metro daily and peruse the general news and business news sections: almost all will have two or more of these attributes.

In addition to the news thread through the story, it wants to include information about the person/company/event: the who, what, when, where, why and how. Ideally, it should also include 'facts and stats' that help support the main story and put it into context.

For a small business success story, for example, it's a good idea to include some background information on how the business owner came to be where they are and what influences or mentors they had.

What do they attribute their success to? What ups and downs have they had along the way? What advice can they give to others?

In writing an article for the media, you must write to the audience and craft the article as if you are the reader. Think what would interest you if you were reading it. That is what the editor or reporter does and you must do the same.

Ask the right questions

So it comes down to asking the right questions of the person or people you need to interview so you can write such a piece.

Firstly, it pays to research the person and company thoroughly beforehand. You should know as much about them as you can. LinkedIn is a great resource for this and the Internet in general.

Secondly, you need to be empathetic during the interview and guide them in a logical way. I prefer a chronological order as this is easier for the person being interviewed and allows you to elaborate or skip over particular aspects of events.

Thirdly, the questions need to relate to the underlying news angle. Often the person may stray from the issue and sometimes you can get some great additional material when this happens, but be mindful to keep the interview on track.

There is an art to writing interesting articles and it does take a while before you become adept at it. There are sure to be one or two gems that come from the interview that can be brought out and highlighted in the heading or introduction.

Ideally you will know the length of your article in advance. Keep in mind it needs to be succinct and doesn't want to contain irrelevant information: make each word count.

PRO TIP: Don't make spelling, typographical or grammatical mistakes as this is a big turnoff for the people who will decide whether or not to publish your article. Ask someone to read or edit the article prior to dissemination.

Chapter 11

Strategic Alliances for Business Growth
by Brenda Thomson

Do you want your small business to grow into a big one?

On your browser search for 'business growth strategies' and I guarantee every search result you find will include **strategic alliances** in the top three ways to achieve rapid business growth.

So what are Strategic Alliances and how can they help to grow your business?

Put really simply, Strategic Alliances are two or more businesses working together on a shared strategy or project to create a WIN/WIN outcome for both of them. There is nothing more complicated to it than that.

Big business has been doing it for years. Think about flybuys reward points. A major alliance strategy between the Coles group of companies and a number of other businesses including AGL, Telstra, Webjet, Best Western, Budget Rent a Car, Jetset ,Travelworld and Medibank Private.

The WIN-WIN? Increased average dollar sale and increased repeat business as consumers shop with the incentive of increasing their reward points; and new customers and repeat business as customers redeem their rewards and generate even more reward points, and the cycle continues.

But it's not just about big business. There are literally hundreds of things that small business owners can do together to achieve business growth. It doesn't matter what kind of business you're in, alliance strategies are only limited by how creative you can be.

Strategic Alliances can be used to generate new leads, increase customer conversions, boost average dollar sales, get your customers coming back more often or referring more clients to you and even reducing your costs.

Here are four simple ideas to get you started...

1. Generating more leads

Strategic Alliances are a great way to generate more leads for your business. By collaborating with other businesses who share your target market you can reduce marketing costs and maximise reach with a whole range of shared marketing and cross promotion strategies. Think about sharing an expo stand, doing a shared letterbox drop, providing articles for each other's newsletters, doing a joint presentation or workshop, even implementing a shared newspaper or radio campaign.

Review all your current marketing strategies and the marketing strategies on your wish list and ask yourself two questions:

- Is this an effective marketing strategy for my business?
- Could I do this more effectively and more affordably if I worked together with another business?

If the answer to BOTH questions is YES then it's time to implement a strategic alliance. (By the way, if the answer to the first question is NO then you shouldn't be doing it anyway.)

2. Improving sales conversions

Strategic Alliances aren't just a great way to generate more leads, they can also be leveraged to generate higher conversion rates than many other marketing strategies. Think about how you can work with other businesses to support each other by sharing attractive and affordable or even free add-ons and bonuses to create irresistible offers and improve sales conversions at the checkout.

And it doesn't stop there. By working with other related businesses you can help each other increase credibility and brand awareness and become recognised as leaders in your field. Think about what you can do to help and support one another: anything from endorsements, reviews and recommendations to sharing articles, co-hosting events and even co-authoring a book.

3. Increasing average dollar sale

As well as improving conversions, Strategic Alliances can help you generate more income at the checkout. We've already looked at the flybuys example of getting customers to buy more in exchange for some form of reward or incentive. For small business owners the best possible way to create affordable incentives and rewards is by working with alliance partners.

But that's not the only way to increase average dollar sale. We are all familiar with the iconic McDonald's up-sell, "Would you like fries with that?" The challenge for many small business owners is that they are often limited to one or two products or services and they simply don't have any 'fries' to offer. Through working with alliance partners you can use someone else's 'fries' and share the profits. Everyone wins.

4. Reducing costs

The benefits of Strategic Alliances don't stop with increasing leads and making more sales. They are a powerful way to reduce costs as well. Savvy small business owners can support one another by forming buying groups, sharing costs and resources, minimising advertising spend and even reducing staff idle time.

Strategic Alliances really are the most powerful business growth strategies available for small business owners. Spend time thinking about it. How can you generate more leads, more customers and more profits in your business by working collaboratively with other business owners?

About the author

Brenda Thomson is passionate about empowering small businesses to create extraordinary businesses through the power of working together. Brenda is the founder and CEO of SMART Small Business Forums, local communities of small business owners working together to help one another through a variety of mutual support and strategic alliance opportunities.

W: www.smartsmallbusinessforums.com.au
E: brenda@smartforums.com.au
P: 1300 790 997
T: @Networkingworld
F: www.facebook.com/SMARTForums
L: au.linkedin.com/in/smartsmallbusinessforums
Y: www.youtube.com/smartforums

Chapter 12

Producing a Newsletter

Before you think about producing a newsletter (for external audiences), you need to determine what its purpose is and whether the effort will justify the reward.

There is considerable work involved in publishing a professional newsletter that is interesting, attractive, error-free, is actually read and works on all levels. It can be one page or 20, but whatever the length, it needs to be written for the reader's interest, not to openly spruik why you are such a great organisation.

While e-newsletters are more typical these days, there is still a place for hard copy newsletters. In fact, I believe that there is such a proliferation of e-newsletters that a hardcopy version may provide a cut-through that is hard to achieve when competing with so much other email.

As part of the planning process, some important questions that you need answers to are:
1. Do you have a database of customers, prospects and other stakeholders or can you create one?
2. Could you buy an opt-in mailing list to add to this list?
3. Do you have someone to manage its production?
4. Can you source enough new information and photos for every issue?
5. How often do you want it come out?
6. Have you got a budget for it?
7. Is there web infrastructure in place to allow for feedback?

8. Have you got a measurement strategy in place to check its success?
9. Will management support it?
10. Do you have someone who can write content and proof material?

If these answers are positive and you believe there will be beneficial rewards in producing a successful newsletter, such as greater brand engagement and more loyal customers, then you are ready to make further investigations.

Other aspects to be part of the planning process include:

- A name for the newsletter.
- Producing a hard copy for distributing to recipients or creating an e-newsletter.
- Developing a template that complements the corporate graphic style.
- Appointing someone to research and write articles and edit others.
- Is this person good at catchy subject lines and keyword placement for SEO (Search Engine Optimisation)?
- Sourcing a photo, graph or illustration to go with each story.
- Appointing someone responsible for its production and meeting deadlines.
- Who will do the graphic design/web uploads/hosting?
- What web analytics software will you use?
- What distribution software will you use?
- Who will be responsible for list hygiene?

There are a lot of boxes to be ticked before deciding to produce a monthly newsletter. It's not easy unless you have a reasonable budget and in-house staff or an external agency who are dedicated to the role. If this isn't the case you could consider a bi-monthly or quarterly newsletter, which still requires staff time and a financial commitment but isn't quite as onerous.

Having hard copy newsletters are great for handing out to customers and prospects, suppliers, new staff, attendees at workshops or seminars, the media and any other stakeholders. And of course, a PDF of the newsletter can be emailed to anyone.

If you don't have a budget for a newsletter in the marketing budget, consider allocating some budget from the sales, HR and corporate departments as they will also benefit from this communication piece.

If you can address all the issues above then you are well on the way to making your regular newsletter get off the ground.

PRO TIP 1: Wondering what stories could be included in the newsletter? Here are some ideas:

- Interesting end user applications
- New products
- Product enhancements/upgrades
- Special offers
- Exhibitions and trade show participation
- Major or unusual orders/contracts
- Profiles of relevant people/companies
- Videos
- Export successes
- New applications
- Tips

- Survey results
- New certifications
- Awards won/nominations
- Any speaking engagements by management
- Milestones reached

PRO TIP 2: To extend the life of your hard copy newsletter, consider not having an actual date to it. Instead you could call it Issue 1, 2, 3, etc. Or if you don't want to be tied down to a particular month, you can call it Spring, Summer, Autumn or Winter edition.

Chapter 13

When is it Time for a New Corporate Identity?

Did you know that visual trends change every decade or so? How old is your logo? Is it current with today's style?

A new identity is like a fresh coat of paint; adding newness and vibrancy. It's also a good excuse for sales people to hand out business cards and flyers with an updated look.

You can also link the new corporate image to a milestone event. For example, in 2012 WMC Public Relations celebrated its 20th anniversary and created a new logo with a different suite of colours and a new tagline.

When considering a logo redesign or refresh, also consider the relevance of your company name and tagline? If it's time to consider this, here are some questions that will help guide you:

1. Is your company name still representative of what you do? Is it descriptive so that people who don't know you would understand what you do purely by reading your company name?

2. Does your logo and tagline reflect your values and what you do?

3. Is your tagline still relevant or have you changed direction since it was introduced? Can it be made more dynamic?

4. Are any of these aspects tired, old fashioned and need to be refreshed and modernised through the use of more up-to-date fonts and colours.

It is also worthwhile talking to your lawyer about the need to trademark your logo and tagline or slogan depending on what it says. Obviously a generic one can't be registered.

Let's look at WMC Public Relations as a case study (note that although these logos are only shown here in black & white, they are colour logos):

OLD:

NEW:

A. The name still describes what the company does and it is well established and respected in the marketplace, so we decided not to change the name.

B. The original logo used traditional fonts and classic colours that were very corporate and professional, but lacked movement and vibrancy. We wanted our logo to indicate we play an active role in social media and introduce warm earthy tones that reflect the colours of Australia's environment, which we are passionate about.

C. The old tagline (The Communication Specialist), while still relevant, needed some pizzazz. So we looked at what we offer clients and broke it down into three key words.
   • Strategy, for the strategic advice we offer clients and the strategies we develop to create PR programs.
   • Action, which demonstrates implementation of PR and publicity programs and that we are proactive.
   • Results, because that is the basis of everything we do; ensuring we obtain results for clients.

If you decide to freshen your corporate identity, choose a graphic designer you are happy with and who understands your business. Make sure he/she provides examples of how the logo and tagline will be applied: for example, on vans and trucks, signage, stationery, websites and social media.

Ask your team and other stakeholders: does it have high impact visually? Can it be recognised easily (in large and small formats)? Is it attractive?

Once you have decided on a new corporate identity, ask the designer to supply the logo in various formats for use on black/white or coloured backgrounds.

While most organisations won't need a detailed style manual, you should make sure the graphic designer supplies the logo in Adobe Illustrator format (.ai) as this is what publishers and printers require. JPEG (.jpg) files are acceptable for many applications but limit how the logo can be applied. .png and .eps files are the most commonly used files that can be saved with a transparent background, but programs such as Word and Excel don't always recognise these file formats.

PRO TIP 1: Ensure the logos are stored safely and you have back up copies.

PRO TIP 2: If you are celebrating a milestone such as 10, 20, 21, 30 or 50 years of business, create a special anniversary logo that can be used with your existing logo. Here are a couple that WMC Public Relations created for its clients (shown in black & white, but actually created in colour):

Chapter 14

Corporate Social Responsibility

What is Corporate Social Responsibility (CSR) and what CSR initiatives can you implement in your business?

In this chapter we provide examples of two businesses that have firm CSR policies and practices in place. Do you have a CSR policy? Is it up to date?

From Wikipedia, the definition of CSR is... "a form of corporate self-regulation integrated into a business model".

CSR policy functions as a built-in, self-regulating mechanism whereby a business monitors and ensures its active compliance with the spirit of the law, ethical standards and international norms.

The goal of CSR is to embrace responsibility for the company's actions and encourage a positive impact through its activities on the environment, consumers, employees, communities, stakeholders and all other members of the public sphere who may also be considered as stakeholders.

If CSR is not already entrenched in your organisation, it should be. All areas of your business should comply, including:

- Workplace safety and employee training
- Product development and materials sourcing
- Packaging
- Product performance

- Pollution control and waste management
- The complaints process
- Advertising and marketing
- Community service obligations
- Corporate philanthropy

By way of example, two companies that take CSR seriously, along with their employees, and who really do contribute to society are Tasty Trucks and Cummins.

Tasty Trucks: Colin Lear established Tasty Trucks in 1989 and since then they have been providing morning tea and lunch to factory and office workers through their mobile vans service. In recent times, more than 15,000 people a day were served via their fleet of vehicles.

For more than 15 years, Tasty Trucks has been donating vast quantities of sandwiches, rolls, pies, salad packs, cakes and other freshly prepared meals to St Vincent de Paul Society's soup vans, which go out every night to feed Melbourne's homeless.

The community also benefits from Tasty Trucks in another important way with employees volunteering as part of a monthly roster system to help out in the soup vans.

This is commendable CSR.

Taking it one step further, Colin has upgraded the vans so they utilise the energy from the engine to heat water that keeps the ovens hot. The fan forced ovens also have a gas assisted burner. The vans and the refrigeration system run on propane gas, one of the cleanest fuels available. This makes for a very energy efficient and environmentally clean vehicle.

Using the knowledge Colin and his team gained in developing their vans, Tasty Trucks has also been instrumental in helping St Vincent's design and build their soup vans which fully comply with the requirements of food handling laws.

That is a perfect example of CSR.

Cummins: Leading diesel engine supplier, Cummins, introduced Community Involvement Teams (CITs) as part of its CSR program. Its CSR mission is to make people's lives better by serving and improving the communities in which Cummins does business, and providing the tools and means for people living on the edge of society to overcome the barriers they face.

Cummins delivers on this core value through its CITs, which serve as an organised employee-driven structure through which CSR work is carried out in the local community.

The CITs select projects based on local community concerns and with a focus on people and groups who are marginalised in society. The Cummins CIT in Scoresby (a Melbourne suburb) chose to partner with three local community not-for-profit organisations: Riding for the Disabled (RDA), Wesley Do Care (WDC) and Hand Brake Turn (HBT).

RDA provides horse riding and related activities for physically and intellectually disabled people of all ages. The program has therapeutic, developmental and social value for the riders. For a few hours each week, several Cummins Scoresby volunteers assist by leading the horses and interacting with these special riders.

WDC provides services for socially isolated people, who are housebound and rarely have visitors. Staff at Cummins Scoresby volunteer their time to do home visits with these often elderly and isolated residents. The volunteers provide company and assist with odd jobs.

The Cummins-sponsored HBT program focuses on further education for local youth at risk with a specific focus on Certificate 1 in Motor/Engine Mechanics, and potentially Diesel Technician apprenticeships. These young people have an opportunity to meet and mix with Cummins volunteers, who share similar automotive and technical passions.

The company encourages and gives all employees an opportunity to participate in community involvement activities on a voluntary basis.

Through Cummins' CSR program, the company seeks to achieve a lasting and positive impact on its local communities.

PRO TIP: Create a leadership team within your company involving all levels of personnel to implement or fine-tune your CSR policy.

Chapter 15

Thought Leadership

If you run a successful business or are a senior executive in an organisation then you presumably have expertise at something.

Thought leadership is where you share your knowledge and opinions on subjects for which you are qualified. It could be on how to operate a successful business or it could be about your speciality or industry you work in. It is one of the key tools used by the PR professional.

One reason for being a thought leader is to raise your profile and your brand's profile and be seen as an authority. If someone is looking for your products or services they have more confidence in purchasing from you/your company. Another good reason is if you are looking for a new job.

To be seen as an authority or thought leader, you should write authoritative articles that relate to topics that are currently being discussed and answer questions being asked.

Added credibility for your thought leadership piece is automatically provided if it is published by a third party. Your article should be tailored to the publication/website you are offering it to and it should be provided to them exclusively (unless it is world shattering when you could distribute it more widely).

So how do you share your knowledge and provide content aimed squarely at your target audience? Let's look at some areas where you can do exactly this:

1. Blogs are an excellent way to demonstrate your thought leadership, either on your own website or as a guest blogger on a site that covers the subjects you are writing about.

2. Commenting on forums is another way you can communicate your leadership to others who have a similar interest. It is certainly one of the areas where you can see what people are talking about and what questions are being raised.

3. Write letters to the editor, primarily of national and metro newspapers. If responding to a previous story in the paper, state the story headline and date published and then give your point of view or opinion, which can be supported by statistics, trendlines and other metrics.

4. Write op-ed pieces (opinion editorials) for newspapers and online publications in response to a story they have published.

5. Many articles published on websites and online forums provide an opportunity to comment, which is another way to add your thought leadership position. Rather than a longer op-ed piece, edit your key messages and communicate them more succinctly.

6. Most thought leadership is business-to-business, so LinkedIn is a good place to a) monitor conversations for topical issues and b) post a comment, making it as controversial as you can to attract attention. To support your comment, you can link it to a fuller-length article, perhaps written as a blog on your website (which is good for driving leads to your website).

The size of a thought leadership article can vary from around 500 to 1500 words. Make sure you have a good quality and high resolution photograph of yourself to accompany the article if it's requested.

Writing a thought leadership piece can require quite a bit of effort, so if you are offering it to a media outlet, it is useful to check with them if they will consider your submission before you start it. If they are interested, they will usually provide you with guidelines and the number of words they require. Don't forget to ask for a deadline and give yourself plenty of time to not only write it, but have someone else read it for relevance.

The key to any thought leadership article is to make it interesting, accurate and relevant to the people who are going to read it.

PRO TIP 1: Ask your PR person (in-house or external) to proof the article before it is published.

PRO TIP 2: An alternative to writing an article is to create a video, which is equally as effective, perhaps even more so if the quality of the video and presenter are excellent. But getting videos published on third party sites is more difficult.

Chapter 16

What is Customer Delight?
By Danielle Storey

My husband David and I have been running a successful business for more than 15 years in an industry where our competitors are all playing the price competition game, so naturally we knew early on that we needed to offer more than just the 'best price in the industry'.

We believed that customer service was going to make a difference. And it did, it just wasn't enough.

Customer service is picking up the phone with a smile in your voice, doing the things that you say you are going to do, turning up for appointments on time and making sure that your paperwork is always in order so that the customer is not inconvenienced.

Five years of offering great customer service didn't get us as far as we wanted because our competitors were smartening up and offering timely service, friendly online websites and still offering cheaper pricing than us.

We decided to create and implement a Customer Delight philosophy and a series of systems in our business. This, we knew was something that our competitors couldn't offer as they were too busy and too financially tight (with very small margins) to get it right. Not only did we focus on delighting our customers, but on delighting our staff, suppliers, each other and ourselves.

Today our business is in the top 10 in the industry in the eyes of the customer, staff and suppliers. Financially we are free to live and love a fabulous lifestyle. This we attribute to Customer Delight.

The very foundation of Customer Delight is the honest, healthy and giving relationship that a company builds with their customers, staff, suppliers and contractors to ensure that everyone wants to continue the relationship.

Mother Teresa said:

"Being unwanted, unloved, uncared for, forgotten by everybody, I think that is a much greater hunger, a much greater poverty than the person who has nothing to eat."

In our western society, Customer Delight is rare. Think about the last time that you were truly delighted by a company. What did that feel like? And more importantly, did the company delight you the second and third time that you used their service or bought their product? When did you feel wanted, loved and cared for by someone you bought a product or service from?

Whether in a personal relationship or a business relationship, every person on the earth wants to be rewarded for their attention, praised for their decisions and acknowledged for their contribution. If it makes you, the consumer, feel great and become a loyal and raving fan, why don't more companies focus on Customer Delight — on wanting, loving and caring for you — their customer?

Funnily enough, the reason most businesses don't actively reward you for your attention has nothing to do with money. Mostly it has to do with a lack of time, and an ignorance of where to start.

The five main reasons you, the existing customer, gets ignored are:

1. **Leaders don't focus on the right priorities**. Many leaders, business owners and managers are busy working *in* their businesses instead of *on* their businesses. They are using their physical energy inefficiently. Many don't know who to or how to delegate to others so that they can find valuable time to become clear about their aims and the systems that are required to put them into process.

2. Most businesses in western society are **more focused on attracting new customers than looking after the ones they already have**. Marketers and advertisers make it easy to buy client attraction strategies that promise the world and rarely deliver it. It is acceptable today that a marketing activity may or may not produce results, regardless of the price to implement it.

3. Many **businesses owners and leaders are frightened of 'getting it wrong'** and therefore don't start a process until they can be assured of its success. Unfortunately, like having children, there are no definitive rules for 'getting it right' and a GET ON WITH IT and BRING IT ON attitude, mixed with a healthy dose of clarity and preparation, will reap more results than endlessly waiting for the right moment. As Paul McCarthy, the great Australian marketing specialist says, 'Fail Faster' to succeed quicker.

4. **There are no systems in place** to ensure that the things that need to happen to delight customers happen, every time.

5. **Business leaders do not know their WHY.** Whether Delighting a customer, rewarding a staff member, implementing a Delight System or any other initiative, do you know your WHY? Do you know your underlying reason for getting up every day and making the decisions and undertaking the activities that you do? If you do you are amongst a small group of people destined to achieve your aims and have success in all that you choose.

Creating truly Delighted customers is not an art or a science; it's simply a series of systems that you can implement easily and maintain consistently. Implementing Customer Delight systems will bring you business rewards regardless of the industry you serve or the product or service you sell.

About the author

Danielle and her husband David Storey, own and operate The Cartridge Family, which sells printers, inks and toners across Australia. Danielle is also a professional speaker, sharing the principals of Customer Delight and Customer Engagement to audiences throughout Australia on the subject of Million Dollar Relationships.

W: www.milliondollarrelationships.com.au
   www.thecartridgefamily.com.au
E: Danielle@Daniellestorey.com
P: 1300 186 637
T: @DanielleJStorey
F: www.facebook.com/MillionDollarRelationships
L: www.linkedin.com/in/daniellestorey

Chapter 17

How to Maximise Your Brand's Presence at Live Events

Your company is one of more than one hundred exhibitors at an event that is attracting tens of thousands of people. How do you stand out from your fellow exhibitors? What can you do to make your brand memorable so that it is recalled after the visitors have left the building, let alone make an enduring connection with you?

By just asking these questions and exploring the opportunities, you are bound to be ahead of half of the other companies there. To get ahead of the other half requires planning and innovative thinking.

In this chapter we look at some ideas that will help put you at the top of the ladder.

First, you need to let people know you are going to be at the event in advance and tell them what they can see or receive from you. What you have to offer wants to be interesting enough and have sufficient an incentive for prospective visitors to take notice and take action.

Fine-tune the messages you want to communicate so that they are consistently mentioned in all areas of the PR and advertising campaign to promote your participation.

Assuming you have a database, you will promote your participation via email, newsletters, on the website, via video, and if you have the budget through paid advertising (pay per click or impression, sponsored stories, banner, print, etc.).

You will send out media releases to online and print publications to meet their deadlines.

You need to use social media to communicate these messages, use photo sharing sites and request Likes and retweets so that a buzz is created around your stand/space.

So what can you do to create this buzz? Some ideas include:

1. Have a celebrity or expert/pro come on your stand who can answer questions, sign autographs or have their photo taken with visitors.
2. Have a fantastic giveaway with visitors required to register on the stand to be in running to win it. Perhaps you could use the latest technology such as blippar to create a point of difference. Check to see if you need to organise a lottery permit as each state has different rules.
3. Have well-branded samples available to give away or a small useful gift. Even a bag of lollies can be used inventively to ensure your brand is made more memorable.
4. Include a learning lounge, lab or theatre adjacent to your stand.
5. Have a teleconference on the stand with interstate people who can't make it.
6. Offer a special and attractive discount for people who visit you.
7. Make the process of entering the competition/giveaway unique or unusual/quirky.

8. Make it easy for people to 'tell a friend' so they just have to make a few mouse clicks. And use the standard 'the more people you tell, the more chances you have' offer.
9. Think outside the box as to what will attract people to your stand and make your presence at the event go viral.

Don't forget that you also want everyone who visits you to be added to your database, so that the next time you have an announcement you have a far greater reach.

If you've followed the advice above, at this stage, you've promoted your event in advance and continued to issue updates at various stages to keep potential visitors engaged. Also, work with the organiser and discuss ways in which you can help them promote the event itself. For example, most organisers send out regular emails to their (usually enormous) database to attract visitors and would welcome a product that they can offer as a giveaway and incentive to help them gain pre-registrations and sell tickets in advance.

So the day has arrived and the event is live! How do you maximise your brand's presence? Well, your stand must be attractive to your desired audience, it wants to be interactive and it needs to deliver on expectations. Ideally, it should give visitors more than they expected.

Use social media throughout the event to post photos and comments that show off the brand. You have presumably created a buzz around your stand and should encourage visitors to tweet and post photos to their social media sites.

What you do on the stand should necessitate further engagement with the people who took the time to visit you. For example, you can send an email announcing a winner if a competition was run on the stand or any other results from the event. Don't forget to thank them for helping make it a success. The aim is to extend their experience beyond their attendance at the event.

PRO TIP: Create strong visuals around the event and use extensively such as a new Facebook cover photo, an infographic, Twitter background and invitation. Distinctive imagery will add impact and develop greater engagement with the audience. Of course it wants to be fun and innovative so it is more memorable.

Chapter 18

Why Being Social is More than Just Using Facebook. Well, Kind of...

By Melanie Kydd

Social Drivel recently posted the article, *Who runs your Company's Social Media? Why?*, which made a compelling case for why some small to medium enterprises fail to achieve returns on social media endeavours: they do not give it the time or the expertise it requires, assuming it can be managed much the same way as personal profiles.

For most businesses, social media is being used as a marketing tool and as such, if you're going to use it, you need to use it right. Commitment, a clear plan of attack and pre-determined goals are all key. The following questions need to be continually addressed:

- How much time do I spend on it?
- Do I hire someone specifically to manage profiles?
- Should I outsource?
- How much content do I post? How often?
- How do social media ads work and should I use them?
- What are the best platforms to use?
- What ROI (return on investment) do I get out of all this?

Don't get me wrong, social media is a fantastic tool for SMEs to have at their disposal. Comparatively speaking it's cheap and it serves multiple functions: increasing brand awareness and advocates; allowing direct communication with customers; and serving as a customer care port. But without a clear strategy you will be wasting time and money, and risk damaging your existing brand image.

Which platform is 'best'?

There is no 'right' answer to this. Platform selection is dependent on your business, target market and goals.

However, generally speaking, Facebook is, and continues to be the most popular and prevalent social media platform in Australia. So for sheer exposure, it has you covered.

As a consequence of this widespread use, you are probably familiar with the platform in some shape or form, which means you will be more comfortable using it. Of course, personal use and business use of social media are markedly different in both goals and methods. However, some level of familiarity always helps when defining the starting point of a new venture.

Management and monitoring

Unlike personal social media, where you come and go as you please, business social media doesn't just 'happen'. Presence needs to be constant. And, unlike customer care phone lines, social media is always open. People can view your profiles at their leisure, posting (public) comments whenever it suits them.

A neglected profile can therefore be more damaging than no profile at all, leading to an impression of poor brand management, with unmonitored and unaddressed customer communications prompting an image of poor customer service.

To prevent this, a management and monitoring strategy needs to be drafted prior to profile set up. A timeline that outlines regular updates, advertising campaigns, competitions and offers will ensure that your profile continually engages and encourages activity around the company.

Your strategy should also include clear documentation, which details how employees interact with any business-related social media profiles and a template for handling any negative comments posted.

Finally, whether outsourcing or not, ensure you receive and compile monthly reports detailing reach, growth and interaction, and adjust your strategy accordingly to ensure your presence continues to be compelling.

Apps

Apps in relation to social media are still a relatively new development and can be somewhat hit-and-miss. Facebook custom tabs are the most popular and well-known, and for some industries they provide a dynamic new addition to the well-known page model.

Their most common incarnation is as a competition tab — commonly designed to contain a 'like gate', requiring people who wish to enter to like your page first.

However, the great number of SMEs shouldn't feel the need to pursue apps initially. It can assist in growing a page, but is by no means a requirement for success.

Advertising

Advertising via social media is becoming increasingly popular and is often the key to generating traffic to your social media profiles.

We recommend Facebook pay-per-click over pay-per-impression when setting up social media advertising: i.e. paying for action rather than passivity. However, both options allow for extremely powerful targeting (demographics, location and interests) and post-campaign analytics, at a rate often much more competitive than Google AdWords.

So to sum up: it's not all about Facebook. But for SMEs it really is — at least in the beginning. A great foundation to build your social media presence upon, a Facebook business profile can give you an indication of your social media capabilities, market reach and style and then assist you in deciding where to go to next.

About the author

Melanie Kydd is Account Manager at Social Media Team, an Australian owned marketing company specialising in social media strategy, design, campaigns, advertising, management and monitoring. Based in Melbourne, they have been providing effective, efficient and affordable social media services for businesses since 2010.

W: www.socialmediateam.com.au
E: info@socialmediateam.com.au
P: 1300 753 393
T: @MelanieKydd & @yoursocialteam
F: www.facebook.com/SocialMediaTeam.FB
L: au.linkedin.com/in/melaniekydd/

Reference:
Who runs your Company's Social Media? Why?
By Chad VanCalster, 23 May 2013
http://www.socialdrivel.com/social-media/item/107-who-runs-your-company-s-social-media-why?

Chapter 19

The Fundamentals of SEO
By Jim Stewart

Search engine optimisation (SEO) is the process of helping your web pages get found by the search engines for certain phrases. The difference between being no.1 or no. 5 for a certain phrase can mean the difference between being in or out of business.

Avoid SEO tricks

A lot of businesses have tried to trick Google in the past by using certain techniques. Sometimes they work and sometimes they don't. One thing is certain though; they do not work in the long term. Google is constantly updating the way it detects webmasters trying to trick it. When it does find sites that violate its rules they disappear pretty quickly from the search results.

The fundamentals of SEO are also the basics

There is no need to trick Google. Think of good SEO like good document structure. Name your document using keywords to give the reader more information about what to expect. For example, I named this chapter the-fundamentals-of-seo-jim-stewart.doc. So when readers open the document, they know what it is about. The same should apply to the names of your webpages and images.

Use your keywords in them so the search engines know what they are about. The opening heading of this document is formatted as a 'Heading 1' and once again it has my keywords in it.

The same should apply to your web pages. At the top of each page have a heading with your keywords in it. This heading should use the H1 formatting. Also name sub-headings known as H2. On a web page you also have an element called a 'Page Title'. This is the first piece of information that Google sees when it crawls a web page. Once again this should include your keywords and be unique.

SEO for images

Not only should your image filenames contain your keywords but you should also include captions where you can, and use your keywords there too. The search engines don't understand images so you have to tell them what they are about. Be descriptive with filenames and captions and use your keywords.

Backlinks and SEO

The thing that made Google a better search engine than all the others was that it looked at what web pages were backlinking to other web pages and used that as a vote for those web pages. The more high quality backlinks a page has, the more authority its content has.

Think of it like an academic paper. If a paper references other papers it gives those papers more authority. You should look to get backlinks from other sites that your audience would frequent. I suggest you offer to produce content for those other sites; whether they are forums, blogs or news sites.

SEO health

Google does not want to send its users to sites that are slow or confusing. Google looks at things like how fast your site is as well as how easy it is for a user to understand. If your site is full of errors or has a lot of duplication with things like page titles or content it will downgrade your site in search results. The best way to monitor these aspects is with Google Webmaster Tools. This is a free service that Google provides.

Keyword discovery for SEO

If you get your keywords wrong then all the above is pointless. You need to understand what words your audience is typing into the Google search box and target those.

A good place to start is to ask family, friends, colleagues and customers the following question. "If you were looking for a product or service like mine, what would you type into Google." It's important to make sure this question is generic and devoid of any keywords. Otherwise you will influence the result. The answers may surprise you.

Once you have some phrases, the next step is to check their search volumes and look for related searches. A great free tool for this exercise is Google Trends. You will not only discover the relative search volumes between phrases you will also see things like geographical popularity and seasonal trends over time. You can then use these phrases as the basis of your content structure.

Search marketing is for people who don't know you

Think of search as the replacement of the old paper directories. People went to them when looking for a product or service, not a brand. If people already know who you are they can find you.

Search is powerful because you appear in front of the user at the exact moment they are looking for your product or service, unlike display, TV or radio advertising. Those old forms of advertising are constantly trying to get their message in front of you when you are not looking for it.

About the author

Jim Stewart formed StewArt Media in 1998 to focus on the emerging area of rich media on the Internet. His expertise in the online space has been greatly sought after by both private enterprise and the public sector. Jim leads a team of people and is responsible for designing and implementing search marketing strategies for clients. The company's focus is not just high rankings in Google but moves beyond that to increasing leads and conversions from sites.

W: stewartmedia.biz
E: info@stewartmedia.biz
P: +61 3 8545 5900
T: @jimboot
F: www.facebook.com/jstewart
L: www.linkedin.com/in/jimboot
Y: www.youtube.com/jimboot

Chapter 20

Melbourne's Urban Forest Strategy
City of Melbourne
Highly Commended in the PRIA Golden Target Awards, Environmental Category

Executive summary

Melbourne is Australia's 'garden city', but after 10 years of drought and severe water restrictions the City of Melbourne's tree population was in a state of unprecedented decline. Over 40 per cent of the city's trees were forecast to be lost from the landscape within two decades. A changing climate, new diseases and the pressures of a growing population were also threatening Melbourne's urban forest. In 2011, the City of Melbourne's Urban Forest Strategy was developed to respond to this situation.

Community understanding of the challenges facing the forest and support for the Strategy was not guaranteed. Would the public misinterpret the organisation's intentions as had occurred with other local government areas managing similar issues?

The organisation developed a campaign, tied to the release of its draft Urban Forest Strategy and the opening of public consultation in November 2011. The campaign aimed to build public understanding of the challenges facing Melbourne's urban environment and gain support for the plan to protect it.

This visually based, participation focussed campaign, drew on a mix of traditional and new communications channels alongside community engagement techniques to help connect with the community, tell the story and establish a joint agenda for the protection of Melbourne's trees. The results were almost entirely positive, initiating discussion, eliciting many responses and widespread support, which helped recognise the critical importance of the urban forest, the need to adapt to climate change and establish the City of Melbourne as the trusted guardian of its trees.

Situation analysis

Melburnians love their trees and open spaces. For decades we have prided ourselves as the garden state. Our iconic parks and tree-lined boulevards are a major part of our heritage and identity.

But after a decade of drought and severe water restrictions it was clear that our garden was not doing too well. Weather conditions, combined with disease and the pressures of a growing population, meant the city was set to lose a quarter of its trees in a decade and almost 40 per cent within 20 years.

As custodian of more than 70,000 trees, the organisation recognised the need to act immediately to make sure that the trees and landscapes - the urban forest – could survive and thrive in a changing environment. The City of Melbourne's Urban Forest Strategy was developed as the city's tree plan for the future, ensuring a diverse, resilient and healthy urban landscape.

The strategy was recognised by academics, scientists and other experts as a vital requirement to build resilience for the future of Melbourne's tree population but it offered solutions that were likely to be contentious with the community, particularly around the need to diversify tree species.

While the plan advocated an increase in canopy cover from 22 per cent to 40 per cent by 2040 to reduce the city's temperatures by four degrees alongside actions to ensure 90 per cent of trees were healthy, there was a risk that these laudable aims might be forgotten for a debate on species selection. Melbourne's communities have very specific preferences for tree selection, often opposed between 'exotic' heritage trees and native trees. The City of Melbourne's Urban Forest Strategy, advocating diversification in Melbourne's tree stock, met neither preference. This was coupled with ongoing scepticism about the City's motives in tree management. In the past, routine tree removals had turned into battles. With the Strategy, the organisation had a serious proposition to make to its residents, businesses and visitors about its future trees. Success rested on robust community engagement.

Goals and objectives

Goal:
Garner community support for the strategy by building understanding of the challenges facing Melbourne's urban forest and the critical value of healthy urban landscapes.

Communication objectives:

1. Understand the community's thoughts and perceptions about the urban forest.

2. Raise community understanding and awareness of the value and necessity of a healthy urban ecosystem for a liveable city.

3. Enable the community to participate in the decision making for City of Melbourne's long-term plan to protect the urban forest and build resilience for the future, linked to a changing environment and population growth.

4. Assist stakeholders understand the reasoning behind the City's preferred approach on tree selection and replacement activities.

5. Gain community endorsement for the Strategy.

Research and analysis

Significant research into the environmental and public health benefits of the urban forest informed the development of the Urban Forest Strategy. The organisation's urban landscape branch had also conducted regular surveys and hold regular community meetings with residents and workers to understand their uses of green space and their preferences. This information informed the approach.

- Melburnians are passionate and vocal about their trees and tree removals have long been a highly sensitive community issue. We also knew about other situations - in Canberra and in Newcastle - where tree removals had ended badly, reflecting negatively on local government bodies.

- Conversations with communities around climate change are difficult. The Strategy was strongly framed around a response to predicted climate change and it required the community to accept that climate change would create vulnerability for the forest unless actively managed.

- A vigorous 'native vs. exotic' tree debate had been running in Melbourne for decades. Groups already existed with stated interests in local areas and specific species.

Target publics

While the organisation was already well acquainted with many stakeholders, it needed to undertake a stakeholder analysis specific to the project. City of Melbourne has a community engagement framework that directs how community engagement activities are undertaken. The framework is underpinned by IAP2 and was employed through the planning process to identified stakeholders and analyse potential impacts.

Key target publics included:

- Residents and resident associations
- Businesses and precinct associations
- Workers

- Visitors
- Developers
- Community interest groups and peak bodies: parks, health, heritage
- State government
- Neighbouring councils
- Universities and academics
- City of Melbourne Councillors, managers, committees and contractors

Communication strategy

The communications campaign emerged from our detailed analysis of each stakeholder group. It was designed to deliver an integrated communications approach where existing community engagement planning tools informed and directed the choice of messaging and the selected communications channels.

The approach rested on three main directives.

1. **The initiative would not be seen as just 'green'.** It would be presented in a way that demonstrated impact across many aspects of life in the city. The strategy was about mitigating and adapting to the impacts of climate change and managing tree diversity and selection, but this desire to create 'forest in a city' also had significant community health and economic benefits.

2. **The story needed to be told visually.** To build a meaningful understanding the organisation needed to distil complex scientific and arboricultural information so that people could

easily grasp the fundamental concepts. Images played a large part in telling the story of Melbourne's evolution. Visualising the loss that would occur, as well as ideas of a future legacy would frame this as an investment in the future - "Making a great city greener".

3. **The story needed many voices.** External advocates were engaged from across the community to support the strategy and actively share the story in order to build momentum. Advocates ranged from a diverse cross-section of prominent Melburnians.

Implementation

The launch

A formal media launch was organised in early November. A transparent community engagement web portal went live, a video was released and a series of events was announced to connect directly with the community. These kicked off in November 2011 when more than 130 people attended a town hall event to learn about the strategy, discuss it and provide feedback. Location specific events were held from January to May 2012.

Maintaining momentum

To enable the community a genuine opportunity to understand the strategy and provide feedback before the strategy was sent to Council to be adopted, it was decided that the campaign should span a reasonable period of time in order to be meaningful and inclusive.

This posed a challenge for maintaining momentum. A set of online tools served as a campaign landing spot. Social and traditional media were used to keep the story evolving. This was supported by proactive media pitches and an Avant postcard campaign through the city's cafés, featuring an illustration by leading artist, Michael Leunig.

Tools and tactics included:

- www.melbourne.vic.gov.au/urbanforest - web portal providing background information, promoting related events and activities.

- www.melbourneurbanforest.com.au - online community engagement portal.

- Video: http://www.youtube.com/watch?v=BplUmxFCE8A

- Events – the strategy was cross promoted through events run by the organisation. It focused on big issues rather than PR. City of Melbourne experts also spoke at a number of external events.

- Media – followed a targeted and adapted approach. The focus was on major metro and niche outlets. A media launch was held with the Lord Mayor and stories pitched over the entire engagement period.

- Social media – various City of Melbourne Twitter and Facebook channels were used and regularly promoted updates on ways to engage.

- Supporting collateral:

  - video
  - infographic
  - series of illustrations depicting before and after scenarios and projected images of the city, thermal images
  - detailed Q&As shared through the organisation for cross promotional opportunities
  - Avant card drawn by cartoonist, Michael Leunig.

- Many ongoing conversations with residents and advocacy groups.

Telling the big story

Related projects were used alongside the Urban Forest Strategy to tell the big story, show connections and demonstrate long term commitment to our urban landscapes.

- The launch of the city's first Open Space Strategy – a plan for the future of our parks and gardens helped tell the bigger story about plans for the city's future.

- The launch of the Exceptional Tree Register continued the story about all the city's trees by asking people to nominate significant privately owned trees for preservation.

- The Urban Forest Art and Design competition engaged the wider community - old and young - in visualising the forest of the future. Winning entries were displayed through the city in November and December, cross promoting the urban forest consultation.

- Even Christmas took an 'urban forest' theme, with the city's Christmas campaign for the city building an enchanted forest to cross promote the urban forest work.

Results

- Urban Forest Strategy document downloaded more than 800 times

- Almost 7000 corporate website hits, with 5,000 unique views

- 11,000 to the engagement portal; 20,000 page views

- 177 web commentators, writing 19,000 words

- Over 4000 video views

- 350 event attendees

- More than 30 media clips, including articles, letters and editorials in the Age and Herald Sun, TV and radio news

- More than 10,000 copies of a specially designed postcard by Michael Leunig distributed to promote the consultation through inner Melbourne

- 419 entrants submitted works for the Urban Forest Art and Design Competition. Winning entries were displayed through the city in November to promote the consultation.

Virtual forum

- 4,249 visitors
- 11,991 site visits
- 20,316 page views
- 1,595 downloads
- 818 UFS downloads
- 177 commentators
- 19,000 words

World café forum

- 135 Participants

Evaluation

The success of this campaign was evaluated in meeting stated objectives.

- The community engagement sessions were well attended. With more than 350 residents, business owners, workers and interested parties attending 10 events we were able to understand existing community perceptions and concerns about our urban forest. This information was fed directly back into the final strategy document. (Objective 1)

- The community forum was very successful in educating people about the situation and process. Surveys of participants showed that prior to the forum 55 per cent of attendees had a basic or no understanding of the situation or our proposal. After the forum this dropped to under 20 per cent, with 80 per cent reporting a good to very good understanding. (Objective 2)

- Considerable, mostly positive, media coverage supported our efforts in reaching broad audiences. The campaign was assisted by a strongly supportive editorial in the Age. Strategy advocates - such as Friends of the Elms - provided an independent voice when negative and/or incorrect information was published. (Objectives 2 and 4)

- Even among highly vocal critics, perceptions changed throughout the engagement period. Some transitioned from blanket opposition to a more nuanced understanding. (Objective 2)

- The Art and Design competition, which attracted more than 400 entries from across the state, was successful in setting the scene for our conversation about the urban forest. Through art we were able to make our proposition tangible and visible and gain access to a wide audience, particularly children. (Objective 2)

- From previous experience, it was expected that eliciting response on a high level strategy would be difficult. But in this case, community appetite was strong. There were high numbers of full document downloads (more than 800), website and engagement portal hits (more than 18,000) and the number of formal submissions received - around 200 formally written and online submissions were more than ever expected. (Objective 3)

- Feedback revealed that the community predominantly supported the strategy. It received widespread academic and industry support locally, nationally and internationally. Almost all commentators expressed opinion about species preference. Only one submission challenged our approach to climate change. (Objective 4)

- Community debate and participation in the engagement process exceeded expectations. Conversations took place in person at events, online through our engagement portal and into the media. An overwhelming number of submissions endorsed the strategy and our approach. (Objective 5)

Note: the PRIA is the Public Relations Institute of Australia, the national industry body for public relations and communication professionals in Australia. Wendy McWilliams is a member of the PRIA: www.pria.com.au

Notes